TAYLOR
MOMSEN

Liz Gogerly

SEA-TO-SEA

Mankato Collingwood London

This edition first published in 2013 by
Sea-to-Sea Publications
Distributed by Black Rabbit Books
P.O. Box 3263, Mankato, Minnesota 56002

Printed in the United States of America, North Mankato, MN

9 8 7 6 5 4 3 2

Published by arrangement with the Watts Publishing Group Ltd, London.

Library of Congress Cataloging-in-Publication Data
Gogerly, Liz.
 Taylor Momsen / written by Liz Gogerly.
   p. cm. – (Teen stars)
 Includes index.
 ISBN 978-1-59771-418-1 (hardcover, library bound)
 1. Momsen, Taylor–Juvenile literature. 2. Actors–United States–Biography–Juvenile
literature. 3. Singers–United States–Biography–Juvenile literature. I. Title.
 PN2287.M66G64 2013
 792.02'8092–dc23
 [B]
                                    2012002539

Series Editor: Adrian Cole
Art Direction: Peter Scoulding
Design: Simon Borrough
Picture Research: Diana Morris

Acknowledgements:
Stewart Cook/Rex Features: 7. Billy Farrell Agency/Rex Features: 28.
Dave Fisher/Rex Features: 23. KPA/ZUMA/Rex Features: 15.
Kraft Foods: 6. Henry Lamb/BEI/Rex Features: 18, 21.
Gregory Pace/Rex Features: 4. Paramount/Everett/Rex Features: 12.
Vaughan Pickhaver/Rex Features: 27. Rex Features: 22.
Tim Rooker/Rex Features: 9. Joe Seer/Shutterstock: front cover.
Sipa Press/Rex Features: 24.
Startraks Photo/Rex Features: 5, 11, 16, 19, 25, 26.
Universal/Everett/Rex Features: 8.
Warner Br/Everett /Rex Features: 13.

RD/6000006415/001
May 2012

Contents

Words highlighted in the text can be found in the glossary.

Momsen Magic!

Taylor Momsen is an actress, model, and grunge rock star. You might know her from the TV show *Gossip Girl*, or you may have seen her on the cover of a magazine. Today you're most likely to find her with her band, **The Pretty Reckless**.

Taylor at the Metropolitan Opera House in 2008.

4

> **"I want to make great records. I want to write great songs. I want to make records for the rest of my life and have each one better than the last, and make myself better at what I do."**

Taylor has been acting since she was three years old. Her first appearance on TV was in a commercial for Shake 'N Bake. At 14, she signed with IMG Models, and went on to appear in magazines such as *Teen Vogue*.

Music has always been Taylor's first love. She's the lead singer with her band, The Pretty Reckless. In 2009, the band went on tour, and in 2010, they released the album *Light Me Up*.

Taylor at her 16th birthday party in July 2009.

Model Child

Taylor Mikel Momsen was born on July 26, 1993, in St. Louis, Missouri. Taylor's mother, Colette, took her to New York when she was two years old to sign with the famous Ford Modeling Agency.

Taylor appears in a TV commercial in 1995.

You can watch Taylor's childhood clips on YouTube. Look for her screen **debut** in the Shake 'N Bake commercial. Also catch her in the 1997 ad for Kraft Singles.

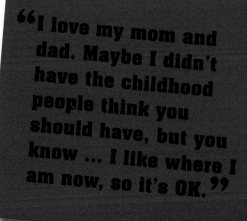

> **"**I love my mom and dad. Maybe I didn't have the childhood people think you should have, but you know ... I like where I am now, so it's OK.**"**

Taylor also began taking dance classes at the Center of Creative Arts in St. Louis while attending Our Lady of Lourdes Catholic Grade School.

She was just a toddler, but Taylor's life in front of the camera was set to roll. "I don't remember what I did on set. I do remember a playroom with puzzles and coloring books."

Taylor, age 9, at the **premiere** of *Spy Kids 2* in Los Angeles, CA.

Little Girl Hits

Big Screen

After the commercials came a few small parts in TV shows, such as *Early Edition* and *Cosby*. However, it wasn't long before Taylor was appearing in movies.

In 2000, at the age of seven, Taylor made her movie debut in the chilling thriller *The Prophet's Game*. Taylor played the part of Honey Bee Swan. It was a minor role, but it was a big beginning!

Taylor alongside the Grinch (Jim Carrey).

Later that year, Taylor was picked from hundreds of other girls to play Cindy Lou Who in the fantasy *How the Grinch Stole Christmas*. She starred alongside Hollywood comic actor Jim Carrey. Many **critics** were impressed with Taylor's performance.

Taylor met Queen Elizabeth II at the royal premiere of *How the Grinch Stole Christmas* in London.

Taylor curtsies as she meets Queen Elizabeth II in 2000.

Rock Solid Roots

Taylor remembers her father taking her to lots of small gigs in St. Louis when she was around eight or nine.

Music was usually blaring somewhere in the Momsen household. Taylor's parents were into classic rock bands such as The Beatles, The Rolling Stones, Pink Floyd, and Led Zeppelin.

Taylor started taking piano lessons, but it was when she picked up the guitar that she found her sound! She formed a band with her sister, Sloane, called Pink Boa. They danced around wearing tutus and masks.

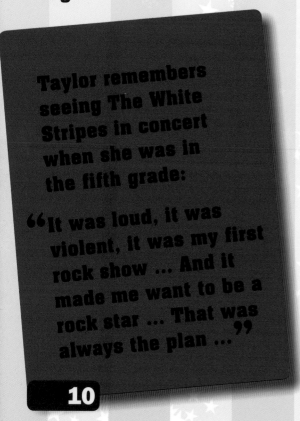

Taylor remembers seeing The White Stripes in concert when she was in the fifth grade:

"It was loud, it was violent, it was my first rock show ... And it made me want to be a rock star ... That was always the plan ..."

Taylor with her little sister, Sloane, in 2007.

Taylor's top rock favorites from the 1990s are: Nirvana—"Heart-Shaped Box," Alice in Chains—"Rooster," Soundgarden—"Jesus Christ Pose," and Rage Against the Machine—"Killing in the Name."

Momsen
at the Movies

Taylor (second from left) alongside her sister Sloane and Mel Gibson (right) in *We Were Soldiers*.

Music may be Taylor's major love, but her breakthrough came as a child movie star.

In 2002, she played the lead girl in the film *Hansel & Gretel*.

Over the next few years, Taylor was regularly cast in family movies such as *Spy Kids 2: The Island of Lost Dreams* (2002), *Saving Shiloh* (2006), *Underdog* (2007), and *Spy School* (2008). She also did more serious dramas such as *We Were Soldiers* and *Paranoid Park*.

During Taylor's film career, she worked with major stars including Julianne Moore, Mel Gibson, Antonio Banderas, and Jason Lee.

But being famous can be lonely. When Taylor did go to school she was teased. She didn't get a chance to hang out or even go out like most normal teenagers do.

> **"I don't really have many friends. I never have. I was always a loner. I was in and out of school so much—so, I dunno, I'm really shy. Which is weird because you probably wouldn't think that."**

Taylor and Jason Dolley in the movie *Saving Shiloh*.

Gossip Girl

In real life, Taylor missed having a normal teenage life. But when she hit TV screens in *Gossip Girl*, she appeared to be living the dream of many young girls.

Taylor got her big TV break when she was 15, in the teen romance drama *Gossip Girl*. The show revolves around the lives of a bunch of rich teenagers living on Manhattan's Upper East Side in New York. The first series hit the screen in 2007. It won Teen Choice Awards in 2008 and 2009, and turned Taylor into a household name with young teens.

In *Gossip Girl*, Taylor played the part of Jenny Humphrey. Jenny evolved from a teenage wannabe to a budding fashion designer.

Taylor filming for *Gossip Girl* in 2008.

Growing Up
on Set

Taylor's time on *Gossip Girl* was exciting and glamorous. There were parties and glitzy awards ceremonies. But the long days filming on set were tiring. Being a star put a strain on her private life, plus she had schoolwork to do.

Filming for *Gossip Girl* in New York, 2009.

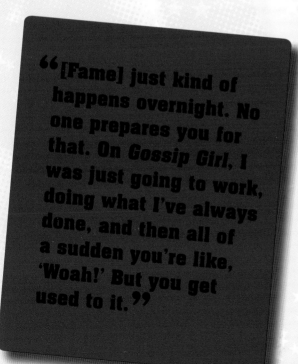

66 [Fame] just kind of happens overnight. No one prepares you for that. On *Gossip Girl*, I was just going to work, doing what I've always done, and then all of a sudden you're like, 'Woah!' But you get used to it. 99

Taylor attended the Professional Performing Arts School in New York for a few years. When that didn't work out, she started taking school lessons on the set of *Gossip Girl*. This often meant doing 20-minute blocks of work between setups.

Eventually, Taylor dropped out of high school two years early. She was bored and didn't see the point: "I'm an artist; I'm not going to use trigonometry." Taylor went on to take college classes online in Language Arts.

Passion
for Fashion

Taylor always had an eye for fashion. Playing a fashion designer in *Gossip Girl* allowed her to dip into the fashion scene.

Taylor and the cast of *Gossip Girl* attended designer shows and fashion events. At one time, Taylor talked about having her own **fashion label**. Her dream collection included simple clothes with a rocker edge.

Taylor and her cover for *Teen Vogue* in 2009.

SEPTEMBER

teen VOGUE

ZY
UTIFUL

in the
clear
what to do
when acne
just won't
go away

FIERCE
FALL
FASHION

Taylor with Madonna (left) and Lourdes Maria Ciccone Leon (center) in 2010.

Taylor's good looks and model figure got her noticed by people in the fashion industry. At 14, Taylor signed with IMG Models. She was one of the youngest girls on their books. As well as being a cover girl for magazines such as *Teen Vogue* and *Seventeen*, she also modeled for John Galliano and Madonna's clothing line, Material Girl.

"I've always been into my own look and love what I wear. When I get dressed up, I always wear what I want to. Fashion is a big part of me, but I always believe it's not what but how you wear clothes."

Rock Revamp

Fans of *Gossip Girl* watched the character of Jenny Humphrey change from fresh-faced schoolgirl to an older, brooding character. In real life, Taylor was changing, too.

One of the first things Taylor changed was her hair. The long locks were given a choppy rock revamp. Taylor also took control of her wardrobe and ditched the pretty frocks. Now Taylor wore a leather jacket and studded shoes to events.

"I had long, pretty hair, and it didn't fit me. I'm pretty, but I'm not, like, a 'pretty girl.' So I pulled up a bunch of photos of Joan Jett and said, 'Do that to my hair' ... it wasn't me that changed—it was just that I decided to start being myself."

It wasn't just Taylor's style that was changing. Taylor was exploring her musical side. For a couple of years, she had been experimenting with her sound with various music producers. She'd also been writing her own songs.

Taylor's image changed as she pushed away from her "schoolgirl" look.

I'm in the Band

Taylor knew she wanted to make loud rock music. She just needed to find the right music producer. In 2008, she met Kato Khandwala.

Taylor and Kato got together with guitarist Ben Phillips and began writing songs. They called the band The Reckless, but later changed it to The Pretty Reckless.

Taylor singing with The Pretty Reckless in 2011.

The Pretty Reckless
in 2010 (from left),
Mark, Taylor, Ben,
and Jamie.

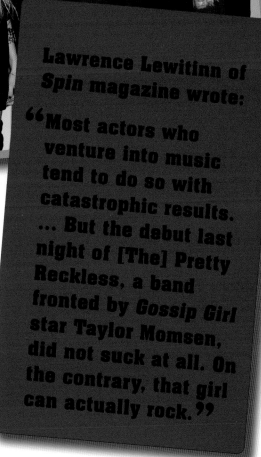

Soon afterward, Mark Damon and Jamie Perkins joined the band. The Pretty Reckless played their first live gig on May 5, 2009, in New York. Lots of people didn't think the Gossip Girl actress had it in her to be a top rock star. With her powerful voice and confident stage presence, Taylor proved the critics wrong.

Light Me Up

In 2009, The Pretty Reckless signed a deal with Interscope Records. The same year, the band toured with Australian band The Veronicas. At last, Taylor's music career was going places.

When Taylor wasn't on the road, she was in the studio writing and recording new material for an album. The Pretty Reckless fans got a taster of the album when the band released its first single "Make Me Wanna Die" in May 2010.

Taylor signs copies of The Pretty Reckless' album *Light Me Up*.

It went to number one in the U.S. rock charts, and made the top 20 in the UK singles charts. A few months later, their debut album *Light Me Up* reached number six in the UK album charts.

"Writing is a very tortuous process, but, you know, I would say one of the most rewarding at the end. But anytime you have an opportunity to play music, whether it's in the studio or on the road, it's the best thing in the world."

Taylor performing at the SXSW Music and Film Festival in 2011.

The Rocking
Role Model

Taylor's style and wild antics on stage have often made her headline material for the wrong reasons. Many upset parents question if she's a **good** role model **for teenage girls.**

The Pretty Reckless started their debut tour in 2010 in the United Kingdom. They went on to perform throughout Europe, the United States, and Asia. Taylor has become a style icon, with her heavy eyeliner, skimpy clothes, trashed black tights, and spiked platform boots.

Taylor's individual style has helped her to stand out from the crowd.

It isn't just Taylor's image that causes concern. Many parents don't like her attitude. Taylor talks openly about sex, and doesn't seem to care what anyone thinks about her.

If her house was on fire, Taylor says she would save her rag doll, guitar, and vintage leather jacket.

"I'm not some cute girl that's been stamped out of a Disney studio and I'm proud of that. Some people like me for it, others hate it. I'm used to that. I've had it all my life."

Where to
Now?

In 2010, Taylor put her modeling career on hold when she left IMG Models. Then the feisty rock chick announced she had quit acting to devote herself to music—she was still just 17.

"I didn't choose acting or modeling, I got thrown into it. I liked it, so that wasn't a problem, but music and songwriting are what I've always really wanted to do."

In 2011, Taylor left *Gossip Girl*. She was grateful for the opportunities the show had given her, saying: "I've had such a great time filming the show."

Taylor at Fashion Rocks in 2008. Now she's left modeling and acting behind.

Right now Taylor is ready to rock on. Some critics focus on her grungy rock-chick side, and think her fame will fade. Meanwhile, many music journalists think she has everything it takes to be a respected singer-songwriter. Time will tell, but right now Taylor believes she's the happiest she's ever been.

Fan Guide

Full Name: Taylor Mikel Momsen
Date of Birth: July 26, 1993
Height: 5 feet 7 inches (1.73 m)
Hometown: St. Louis, Missouri
Record Label: Interscope Records
Color of Eyes: Blue
Hobbies: Dance lessons, movies, and music

There are many, many sites about Taylor, and often they let you contribute to discussions about her. Remember, though, that it's OK to make comments, but it's not fair to be unkind. She cannot answer your comments herself!

http://www.imdb.com/name/nm0597410/

http://www.taylor-momsen.net/

http://www.theprettyreckless.com/#!all

http://www.facebook.com/theprettyreckless

http://twitter.com/#!/tprofficial

taylormomsen.org

taylor-daily.com

http://www.mtv.com/music/artist/momsen_taylor/artist.jhtml

July 26, 1993	Taylor Momsen is born
1996	TV debut in Shake 'N Bake commercial
1997	Appears in commercial for Kraft Singles
1999	Movie debut as Honey Bee Swan in thriller *The Prophet's Game*
2000	Stars as Cindy Lou Who alongside Jim Carrey in *How the Grinch Stole Christmas*
	Nominated for a Saturn Award for Best Performance by a Younger Actor
2002	Appears in *We Were Soldiers*, *Hansel & Gretel*, and *Spy Kids 2: The Island of Lost Dreams*
2006	Appears in *Saving Shiloh*
2007	Takes lead roles in *Paranoid Park* and *Underdog*
2007–2011	Plays the part of Jenny Humphrey in hit television series *Gossip Girl*
2008	Taylor signs to modeling agency IMG Models
	Acts in the movie *Spy School*
2009	Taylor is the cover girl for *Teen Vogue*
	The Pretty Reckless signs to Interscope Records
	The Pretty Reckless performs live for the first time at the Annex in New York
	The Pretty Reckless goes on tour for the first time as support act to The Veronicas
2010	Becomes the face of the store chain New Look
	Madonna selects Taylor as the face of her new fashion line Material Girl
	The Pretty Reckless releases its first album *Light Me Up*
2010–2012	The Pretty Reckless embarks on the Light Me Up Tour. The band tours Europe, the United States, Asia, and Australia
2011	The Pretty Reckless performs at music festivals worldwide including Soundwave Revolution in Australia, Wireless Festival in the UK, and Lollapalooza in the United States
	Taylor announces that she is quitting acting
2012	The Pretty Reckless performs its second headline tour, The Medicine Tour

Glossary

Critics People who are skilled in judging the performances of actors, actresses, dancers, and musicians, and who write or broadcast their opinions.

Debut First public appearance as a performer.

Fashion label A set of clothes designed by a person named on the label, or where a famous person uses their name to promote a certain style of clothing.

Gig Another name for a music concert.

Premiere First public performance of a play or showing of a film.

Role model Someone whom others look up to and want to be like.